IASA Title VI 01-197

MARGARET KNIGHT

Girl Inventor

AMOSKEAG MILLS

MANCHESTER, N.H.

MARLENE TARG BRILL

Illustrations by Joanne Friar

The Millbrook Press
Brookfield, Connecticut

Published by The Millbrook Press, Inc.
2 Old New Milford Road
Brookfield, CT   06804
www.millbrookpress.com

Library of Congress Cataloging-in-Publication Data
Brill, Marlene Targ.
Margaret Knight : girl inventor / Marlene Targ Brill; illustrations by Joanne Friar.
p. cm.
Summary: Describes how Mattie Knight developed her first invention, a stop-
motion device to make looms safer for workers.
ISBN 0-7613-1756-2 (lib. bdg.)
1. Knight, Margaret, d. 1914—Juvenile literature. 2. Children as inventors—
United States—Biography—Juvenile literature. 3. Looms—United States—
History—19th century—Juvenile literature. [1. Knight, Margaret, d. 1914.
2. Inventors. 3. Women—Biography.] I. Friar, Joanne H., ill. II. Title.
T40.K55 .B75   2000
609.2—dc21
[B]   99-045145

Margaret E. Knight was six years old when her father died. He had been
a carpenter in the shipyards of York, Maine. Margaret was beside herself with
sadness. Then the family ran out of money without her father's pay. Margaret's
life turned upside down again.

Margaret and her mother moved to the factory town of Manchester, New
Hampshire. Her older brothers and married sister who lived there promised to
help them. Margaret's family worked for Amoskeag Mills, a giant cotton factory.

Back then, many children in mill towns worked. By 1848, when Margaret
was ten, she worked in the mill, too. Mostly, Margaret cleared the spinning
frame of newly spun thread. She removed the thread-filled bobbins and replaced
them with empty ones.

Mattie, as her brothers called her, didn't mind the heavy loads and
thirteen-hour workdays. What she hated was the cotton fuzz that made her
sick. She had to stay home months at a time just to clear her lungs.

When Mattie was sick, her mother kept her busy with housework. But
Mattie missed the mill. Most of all, she missed the thrill of the machines. As
long as she could remember, Mattie liked to build and invent. She often went to
the mill just to look at how the machines worked, even when she was sick.
Her first-known invention came after one of these visits.

"Margaret, stop fussing with that kite, and take William's lunch to the mill," Mother ordered. She shook her head and let out one of her long sighs. "Why can't you play with dolls like other girls?"

Mattie carefully laid aside the wood frame she was sanding. She grabbed William's pail from her mother. Mattie stuffed it with buttered bread wrapped in newspaper, an apple, and a coffee-filled jug. She never said a word. She just turned with the pail and headed out the door.

"I can't help what I like," Mattie grumbled after the door
shut. "I will always prefer a jackknife, gimlet, and pieces of
wood any day to bits of china with silly faces."

Mattie kicked a rock. It bumped from stone to
stone on the path in front of her. She charged after the
rock until her anger at her mother's stinging words left her.
Then she walked down Pine Street toward the tree-lined road along
the canal. Mattie followed the canal's gentle *S* for almost a mile,
stopping often to catch her breath. Soon a huge family of factory
buildings filled the sky.

Mattie passed under the red brick arch through the tall iron gates. Inside the mill yard, she found the doorway to Number 4. The building stood six stories high and held more than six-hundred looms. Mattie climbed the iron stairs to the second floor where William worked. She felt proud her brother was a second hand, the boss of a large loom room.

Mattie stopped at the top of the stairs to rest. Loud sounds bounced off the hard brick walls. The long weaving rooms were the worst. Endless rows of iron and wood looms filled each room. The thundering roar of their slapping parts pounded in Mattie's head. She could hardly think. When she worked, she got used to the racket. But she had been sickly for some time now. She had forgotten how much noise was part of the job. Even with the noise, the fast-paced looms attracted Mattie like a magnet.

Brightly colored warp threads were fixed to the top and bottom of the loom. Shuttles held the ends of weft, or cross, threads. The shuttle shot back and forth across the long warp threads with lightning speed. Meanwhile, the thumping loom shifted the threads up and down. That way, the shuttle passed over and under the threads, and patterns appeared in the cloth.

Mattie stopped to watch green shuttle thread fly over and under long blue strands. With each pass of the shuttle, blue and green striped cloth formed on the loom like magic.

Suddenly, a shrill scream pierced the sound of the clattering machines. "Get a doctor!" rang excited calls from the next room. Looms ground to a stop around Mattie. Workers pushed through the doorway to see what had happened.

Mattie followed to where the crowd gathered. There was a mix of men, women, and children. A second hand charged through the crowd, clearing a path for Mattie, too. She peeked from behind his wide back. "Oh, no!" Mattie gasped in horror.

Tom, a small boy of about eight, slumped over the loom. A river of blood flowed from his cut-up arm. He bit his lip not to cry.

"Take him to the doctor," the second hand ordered. "Somebody clean this bloody mess. Everyone else back to work." A man scooped up the boy and ran out the door. The crowd scattered slowly.

Mattie shook her head. Each time a thread breaks, the shuttle slips, cutting another worker badly. First her friend Mary; then young Daniel, who died after his accident. Now Tom. No wonder these shuttles are called the "kiss of death." Why doesn't anyone invent a safer machine?

Mattie ran to find William at the other end of the building. She walked with him to the mill yard and stayed while he ate. The story of Tom's accident and the broken shuttle exploded from her lips. She couldn't stop thinking about Tom and the terrified look on his face.

"I've got to try and invent a safer shuttle," Mattie decided.
William smiled at his sister's strong words. "If only you could,"
he said, putting his arm around her.

From that time on, all Mattie thought about was shuttles.
Each day she made sure she delivered William's lunch. Then she
snuck into a weaving room—just to watch.

During noon break, Mattie looked under and over the loom.
She practiced pulling threads in and out. After the second bell,
weavers returned to their looms. Mattie studied how they
threaded and moved the shuttle.

One night Mattie visited her sister, Eliza, and her husband, Charles. He worked in a machine shop like her older brother.

"How do you go about inventing new machines?" Mattie asked Charles.

"Why would you want to know, Mattie?" he asked.

"I'm going to invent something to keep the shuttles from cutting us up," Mattie said boldly.

"Leave machines to the men," Charles scolded. "Many have tried to improve on the shuttle and failed."

Mattie never listened to such talk. "*I* won't fail," she insisted. "Please, please tell me how you go about inventing something in the shop." She kept after Charles until he gave in. He liked her pluck.

"If I were you, I'd start with drawings," Charles said. "Pictures are my map of what to do. Then I build a model from the best drawing. The model gives me moving parts to test my ideas."

What Charles said made sense to Mattie. She often made drawings of her kites and toys before she built them. Now pictures of looms popped into her head. All she needed was time to put them on paper.

Days flew by. Cooking, washing, and ironing left little time for Mattie to invent. Finally, Mattie was able to finish the dinner dishes early. She brought her pencil and journal to a small space under the stairs. This was her special place, her thinking spot. She nestled into the corner and opened the journal to a blank page.

That night Mattie started ten different drawings. Nothing looked right. "If only I could draw a better likeness of a loom, " she sighed sleepily. She closed her journal and went to bed.

Mattie tried again after church the following Sunday. After two or three starts, she checked her drawings and smiled. Each picture looked a little more like a loom. She kept drawing until Mother lit the oil lamps. Mattie's eyes were tired. But she refused to give up. "I'm so close," she said.

Just after midnight, Mattie drew a picture that pleased her. "Now the fun part—building," she said proudly.

The next day Mattie scrubbed her clothes on the washboard in record time. She hung them on the line even faster. Just as she finished, Mother announced she was going out to buy bread.

Mattie saw her chance. She raced to the woodpile and loaded an armful of scraps to carry back to the house. Once inside, Mattie dragged a small table into her thinking spot. She placed a hammer, some screws and nails, and her jackknife and gimlet on the table. She stacked the wood on the floor next to her. Then she sat down, looked at her last drawing, and began her model.

Mattie bore holes into three pieces of wood with the gimlet. She carved one piece into a shuttle and threaded it. The other two became part of the loom frame. After she built a good look-alike, she thought about how to make it safer.

What should I change? Mattie wondered again and again. *Why do I think I can do this? Maybe Charles is right. Maybe I should leave machines to the men.*

But Mattie remembered Tom and the pain on his face. Fixing the loom became more important than anything she had ever wanted to do. "I won't give up," Mattie said, pounding the table.

For days Mattie couldn't keep her mind on housework. She thought about the model while baking pies. She considered different parts as she cut carrots for dinner. If only she could find a way to stop the machine when something went wrong.

"That's it!" Mattie shouted at dinner one night. She spilled her soup down the front of her dress.

"Margaret Knight, pay attention to what you are doing," Mother scolded. "Where is your mind?"

"With the shuttle, Mother," Mattie shouted. "I think I've got it."

Mattie sopped up the soup and hurried from the table to her thinking spot. She uncovered her model and adjusted a spring next to the shuttle. Then she screwed a small piece of wood onto the frame near the spring.

Mattie shoved the shuttle through some warp threads. As it moved, she cut a thread. The wooden bar blocked the spring from moving the shuttle once the thread was broken.

She threaded the shuttle four more times and snipped the thread. Each time the shuttle slipped, the loom stopped. Mattie could hardly wait to show Charles.

"I think you might have something," he said after seeing her test. "I'll know for sure after I try your idea on a real loom." Mattie was thrilled. If only her idea worked. Think of the boys and girls she could keep from harm.

The next day Charles took Mattie's model to the mill shop. Mattie went along to watch. None of the men believed that she had built the model. "Girls and machines don't mix," one man said sternly.

Charles put Mattie's model next to a loom. He moved a spring and added a wooden bar. Now the loom looked like Mattie's model. He broke a thread near the bobbin to test the shuttle. Then he slit another thread closer to the woven cloth. Each time a thread was broken, the machine stopped. The shuttle just dropped where it was.

Charles showed Mattie's invention to Tom Fogarty, the shop second hand. Tom was amazed that a girl knew about machines. "This stop-motion gadget will change weaving forever." He smiled at Mattie. "It will cut the number of accidents. It'll lower the number of broken threads in the cloth."

Charles grabbed Mattie and whirled her around. "You did it," he shouted.

The idea seemed so simple. Yet no one before had thought to stop the machine. It took the strong will and clever mind of a twelve-year-old girl.

Afterword

Amoskeag Mills added Mattie's invention to every loom in the factory. Mattie, however, never received a penny. Companies often kept the patents on inventions made by their workers. Still, Mattie felt good knowing her invention would save countless lives.

Mattie's interest in machines lasted throughout her life. Her inventions touched the manufacture of clothing, shoes, rubber, window sashes, and other household goods. Most inventions applied to heavy machines in factories, and cars.

Mattie's most famous invention folded square bottoms on paper bags. For the first time a bag could stand by itself. This invention earned her the name "Lady in a Machine Shop." To this day, grocery stores worldwide fill bags produced from Mattie's invention.

By the time she died at age seventy-six, Mattie had twenty-seven known inventions. She sold many other inventions to companies where she worked. Mattie's ideas brought her acclaim but little money. When she died, Mattie left $275.05 in the bank, a small amount even in 1914.

But Mattie never seemed unhappy. She lived a full life doing what she liked best—inventing machines. To this day she shines among women for her large number of inventions, especially for heavy machinery. For Mattie, however, her greatest success was a stop for the loom, an invention she created when she was only twelve years old.

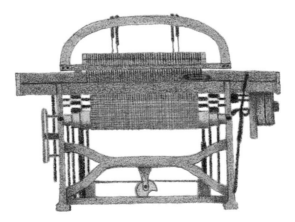

Glossary

bobbin   wooden spool on which yarn is wound; bobbins come in different shapes and sizes, depending upon the use

gimlet   small hand tool for poking holes

mill   building where raw goods are turned into finished products

mill town   factory town

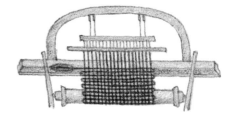

patent   legal grant to an inventor giving that person the rights to make, use, and sell the invention

second hand   boss of a room or section of a factory

shuttle   bullet-shaped handle for carrying cross threads back and forth through long threads on a loom

warp   threads fixed to the top and bottom of a loom

weft   cross threads on a loom